Peter Dela Fontaine GOLDSMITH
At the Golden Cup in Litchfield Street
SOHO. Makes, & Sells all Sorts of Gold & Silver
Plate, Swords, Rings, Jewells &c, at ye lowest prices

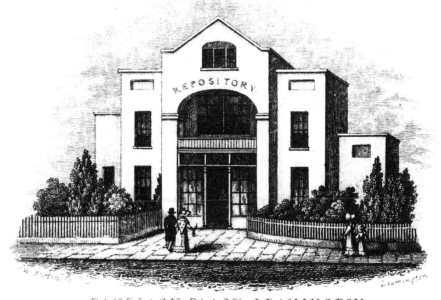

RANELAGH-PLACE, LEAMINGTON.

Jewellery, Silver & Plated Goods, Bronzes, Cabinet Ware, Cutlery, Toys, &c.

An Introduction to

English Silver from 1660

This dish was commissioned by Pugin in 1848, for the sum of £37–15s, as a gift to his
friend Benson who was acting as an intermediary between Pugin and his intended
third wife Helen Lumsden. Unfortunately the marriage never took place because of
severe opposition from the lady's relatives to both Pugin and his Roman
Catholicism.

The surviving day book of Hardman's for 1845-49 describes this piece as: 'A Large
Silver Dish in Florentine pattern, with enamels in Centre of Arms.' It is possible that
its design reflects Pugin's travels in Italy the previous year. He was fascinated by
Florence but repelled by the classical architecture of Rome.

1

A Goldsmith's workshop in the reign of Charles II. Frontispiece to the second edition of *A New Touch-Stone for Gold and Silver Wares,* William Badcock, London, 1679. (15.5 × 8.5 cm)

The Legend:

1 St. Dunstan, the patron of the Goldsmiths' Company
2 The Refining Furnace
3 The Test with Silver refining on it
4 The Fineing Bellows
5 The Man blowing or working them
6 The Test Mould
7 A Wind-hole to melt Silver in without Bellows
8 A pair of Organ Bellows
9 A man melting or Boiling or (an)nealing Silver at them
10 A Block, with a large Anvil placed thereon
11 Three Men Forging Plate
12 The Fineing and other Goldsmiths Tools
13 The Assay Furnace
14 The Assay-Master making Assays
15 His Man putting the Assays into the Fire
16 The Warden marking the Plate on the Anvil
17 His Officer holding the Plate for the Marks
18 Three Goldsmiths, smallworkers at work
19 A Goldsmiths Shop furnished with Plate
20 A Goldsmith weighing Plate

An Introduction to

English Silver from 1660

Eric Turner

Research Assistant, Department of Metalwork
Victoria and Albert Museum

LONDON: HER MAJESTY'S STATIONERY OFFICE

Copyright © Eric Turner 1985
First Published 1985

Series Editor Julian Berry
Designed by HMSO/Graphic Design
Printed in the UK for HMSO

ISBN 0 11 290412 2
Dd 718125 c65

To Flora

ACKNOWLEDGEMENTS

First, I would particularly like to thank Shirley Bury who has provided consistent advice and encouragement, and moreover has been very generous in allowing me access to unpublished material of hers on the 19th century. Other colleagues of mine who have been very helpful are Philippa Glanville, Michael Snodin and Anthony North.

The photography has been undertaken by Mike Kitcatt, who took the majority of the plates, Peter Macdonald and Philippa Williamson.

Finally, I am grateful for the help I have had from Marjorie Trusted, Jane Stancliffe, Jonathan Voak and especially Christine Darby who has unstintingly transformed my manuscript into typescript.

HER MAJESTY'S STATIONERY OFFICE

Government Bookshops

49 High Holborn, London WC1V 6HB
13a Castle Street, Edinburgh EH2 3AR
Princess Street, Manchester M60 8AS
Southey House, Wine Street, Bristol BS1 2BQ
258 Broad Street, Birmingham B1 2HE
80 Chichester Street, Belfast BT1 4JY

*Government publications are also available
through booksellers*

The full range of Museum publications is displayed and sold at
The Victoria and Albert Museum, South Kensington, London SW7 2RL.

The year 1660 is a convenient starting date for the study of the modern period in the history of English silver. A cursory survey of any major collection of English silver, such as in the V&A, will immediately establish that the quantity of antique plate existing from the Restoration is very much greater than that of any period before. There are several reasons for this. Plate, because of the inherent value of the material used, had always been regarded as a convertible commodity. Corporations, the clergy and the landed gentry, those that traditionally enjoyed the financial discretion to invest in plate, found themselves suffering continuous and heavy taxation during the Commonwealth. The heavy military expenditure involved in maintaining a standing army during this

2
(a) Beaker
Silver
Hallmarks for London 1664-5, maker's mark indecipherable
H. 16.2cms. Diam. (of lip) 11.8cms.
51-1879

(b) Porringer and cover
Silver
Hallmarks for 1661-2, maker's mark IW over a tun
Engraved with crest (a hounds head on a coil of rope) on cover and the base with initials S.S.A in a triangle
H. 15.5cms. W. 21cms.
M.11-1963

period put a tremendous strain on the country's resources. The corporate or individual's holdings in gold and silver were usually the first to suffer in the provision of government revenue.

Additionally, a desire to remove the relics and vestiges associated with the previous administration emerged in the first few years under Cromwell, and consequently the Royal Regalia was melted down in 1649. But the corporations fairly quickly realised that they needed plate for their own civic functions and refashioning was not economically possible. The destruction of plate purely for its immediate historic associations slowed down, although subsequently, at the Restoration, the coronation of Charles II was delayed for several months while new pieces were made.

Moreover, during the Commonwealth there seemed little point, when commissioning new plate, in investing heavily in 'fashioning' — the price paid for the goldsmith's work as opposed to the investment in the material itself — when it was likely that the work would soon have to be melted down in response to a new tax demand. This explains to a large extent the relative simplicity of plate produced during the middle of the 17th century. The puritan desire for simplicity, an assumption commonly made to explain the artistic simplicity of much plate produced in the period immediately prior to the Restoration, was merely incidental.

A large scale destruction of plate had also already occurred in the reign of Charles I. His attempt to govern the country without the consent of Parliament quickly led him to fund-raising schemes of dubious propriety if not outright illegality.

Civic corporations and university colleges had enjoyed a period of prosperity prior to the reign of Charles I, and their large holdings of plate were obvious sources of revenue. Just before the battle of Edgehill in 1642 twelve colleges surrendered to the Oxford Mint a total of 1610 lbs 1 oz and 18 dwt of silver. Further individual colleges made hefty contributions to the royalist cause. Exeter, for example, gave 24 lbs 5 oz 1 dwt alone while the contribution from the local gentry and clergy amounted to just over 700 lbs.

Thus political upheavals had a grave and detrimental effect on the goldsmiths. At such times, they were amongst the first tradesmen to suffer and they probably suffered the most. The restoration of the monarchy in 1660 illustrated the axiom that political stability ensures economic stability and therefore a flourishing goldsmiths' trade. Under the reign of Charles II, substantial new quantities of plate were ordered.

The new monarch, during his years of exile, had cultivated luxurious tastes and his life style, on his return, was notable for its extravagant ostentation. Encouraged by Royal precedent, his immediate court circle swiftly followed suit, and they in turn influenced the rising and increasingly prosperous merchant classes. The elimination of punitive taxes on loyalist supporters, the large scale disbandment of the military and the restoration of royal favour dispersed through gifts of plate, stimulated the trade still further.

The commercial and cultural ties between the Netherlands and England during the 17th century encouraged Dutch influence on design in the decorative arts. At the Restoration, with the sudden stimulus to trade, Dutch sources were frequently drawn on and used in the production of elaborate display plate which the English silversmiths had, until then, had little opportunity and experience in providing. Dutch painting illustrates an intense and popular interest in botany and biology which was duplicated in published designs of the period and hence used in English furniture, textile and silver production. Between 1658 and 1670, floral motifs derived from Dutch fruit and flower paintings proved particularly popular. At times animal motifs and more traditional decorative elements were introduced as well from German, French and Italian sources, although the combination of these elements, and hence the final overall design, was usually the work of the English goldsmith.

The richest treatment of these designs was achieved by embossing; that is modelling in relief produced by working with a hammer and punches on the back of a sheet of metal fixed on some yielding material (eg a bed of pitch). Chasing is work on the face of a sheet and is a term also used for finishing up the surface of castings. The required relief forms the structure of the design. Embossing, which had been known to English goldsmiths since the reign of Charles I, proved immensely popular in the years immediately following the Restoration. Despite his cavalier manner towards the Royal Plate collections, Charles I had introduced the Utrecht goldsmith, Christian van Vianen, to the English Court. He stayed between 1637 and 1644 and returned in 1652 to stay another four years. Van Vianen promoted a style of extravagant embossing often using lobular scrolls of indefinite form, and in asymmetrical combinations; it became known (see plate 3) as the auricular style because of its vague resemblance to the gristle of a human ear. The style had few adherents amongst goldsmiths. It required enormous skill and its principal exponents were Christian van Vianen's father, Adam, and the father and son partnership of the Lutmas, again from Utrecht. However, it did prove to be popular amongst discerning and adventurous clients and dramatically demonstrated the limitations and potential of embossing.

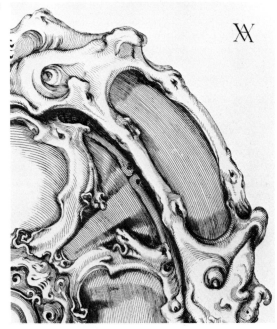

3
Design for the decoration of a dish
Etching
Plate 29 in an album of designs by Adam Van Vianen, *Modelles Artificièls De divers Vaisseaux d'argent et autres Oeuvres,* Published by Theodore de Quessel and dedicated to the artist's son, Christian Van Vianen.
26 × 9.4cm.
24334,28
This plate illustrates the extraordinary fluidity of the auricular style.

As the country became more prosperous in the third quarter of the 17th century, the fashion for finely embossed pieces of silver became well-established. It is impossible now to determine how much plate was manufactured by foreigners resident here and what proportion was produced by English goldsmiths reacting to foreign trends. Those goldsmiths that can be identified as foreigners and resident in London during the early years of Charles II appear largely to be specialists in embossing. But that does not necessarily prove that the technique was always the work of emigrés. Even before he was restored to the throne, the London trade petitioned the wardens of the Goldsmiths' Company, in 1653, to approach Parliament in order to seek restrictions on the activities of the immigrant goldsmiths. They, with new techniques and styles, were steadily increasing their share of the market. The petition failed, and the English goldsmiths were forced to adopt and develop the new techniques themselves, so that they too could compete for the grandest and most lucrative commissions.

Because of the destruction of the Goldsmiths' Company records in the fire of 1681, we are now unable to identify the makers of much of the extant plate made before that date. However, it is possible to be more positive about some of the sources for its design. One of the most popular decorative devices, of acanthus leaves interspersed with putti, was engraved in a series of variations by the Italian Polifilo Zancarli around 1625. French copies appeared in the middle of the 17th century and in 1672, John Overton, a London publisher, re-issued them by collating his own edition from French and Dutch sources. The foreign influence on English design was often already filtered through various countries before it crossed the Channel.

Other techniques commonly employed by silversmiths at the Restoration included matting and flat chasing. 'Matting' or 'pinking' was achieved by the repeated striking of a round headed punch on the surface of the metal, thus creating a myriad of small punched indentations (see plate 5). It was particularly popular throughout the 17th and 18th centuries, and usually used to form a contrasting background for more ambitious, burnished ornament. However in the 17th century, especially when a client requested cheap ornamentation, it was used as a decorative feature in its own right, and for a period competed successfully with more elaborate forms of decoration.

Flat chasing, another traditional technique, emerged as a primary form of decoration in the 1680s. A flat-edged chisel was employed to indent the surface of the metal, producing an effect somewhat similar to engraving although the method of achieving it is fundamentally different. With flat chasing the metal is pressed in, but not removed, whereas with engraving, the surface of the metal is scored and removed with a graver or scorper. Thus engraved ornament provides a crisp pattern while flat chasing creates a softer fuller outline.

Neither form of decoration was necessarily carried out by the goldsmith himself, but was often subcontracted to outworkers specialising in these techniques. The fashion for flat-chased chinoiserie decoration in England during the 1670s and 1680s supports this argument. Chinese porcelain, lacquer and textiles were imported in increasing quantity during the latter part of the century. Not only were the forms of Chinese porcelain copied by English goldsmiths in the production of ginger jars and vases, but surface decoration of chinoiserie scenes was applied to a wide range of objects, as diverse as mugs, tankards, porringers, salvers and toilet services (see plate 6). These depicted Oriental figures,

4
Two handled cup with cover and salver
Silver gilt
Maker's mark only: a star above an escallop with six pellets
London c 1665 (Jackson p.127)
Engraved with the arms of Anthony Ashley Cooper, 1st Earl
of Shaftesbury, impaling those of his wife, Margaret Spencer
Diam. 20.5cms. H. 17.5cms. (porringer)
Diam. 38.5cms. H. 7.5 cms. (salver)
M.104-b-1984
The surfaces are embossed and chased with hunting scenes,
and with borders of auricular dissolving masks, showing the
influence of the work of the Van Vianens and Johannes
Lutma. The lack of a hallmark and the high quality of the
workmanship indicate that this set was probably a special
commission. A porringer and salver, or 'faire state cup' as
Samuel Pepys called one given to him, was a popular gift from
the 1650s until the end of the 17th century
The identity of the goldsmith is discussed in Charles Oman's
Caroline Silver. He was almost certainly a foreign goldsmith
employed on commissions for the Jewel House.

5
Teapot
Silver gilt
Maker's mark only: R.H.
London, c 1685

H. 14.5cms.
M.48-1939
The design is based on that of a Chinese porcelain ceramic
jug; the surface is decorated with 'matted' or 'pinked'
decoration.

6
Toilet service
Silver
No hallmarks; maker's mark S crowned, on five pieces
London c 1680
Bequeathed by Mrs David Gubbay
H. 56.5cms. W. 46cms. (mirror)
M.21-p-1968
This is one of a number of toilet services by prominent
London goldsmiths which are decorated with chased
chinoiserie designs. The motifs appear to be derived from
contemporary prints and descriptions of the Far East
supplemented by European plants and foliage.
A single engravers workshop may have decorated all the
services. This one is reputed to have been given by Charles II
to the Strickland family of Sizergh Castle, Westmoreland.

exotic birds and ornamental landscapes, interspersed
with traditional European decoration. The designs were
doubtless adapted from numerous sources. Precise
attributions are difficult to make although the English
translation of John Nieuhoff's *An Embassy sent by the
East Indian Company of the United Provinces to the Grand
Tartar Cham or Emperor of China,* published in 1669, was
widely circulated and does seem to have been used as a
source for some of these designs. The use of the same
devices and motifs on pieces of silver of different dates,
bearing several makers' marks, suggests strongly that the
goldsmiths sent their work to specialists who had established a virtual monopoly in flat-chased chinoiserie.

The predominantly Dutch influence on English
goldsmiths' work was challenged by the increasing numbers of French Huguenots in London who had begun to

7
(a) Waiter
Silvergilt
Hallmarks for London 1698-9, maker's mark of Benjamin
Pyne (working 1676, died 1732)
Engraved with the arms of Sir William Courtenay of Powder-
ham Castle, Devon; perhaps by Simon Gribelin (1661-1733)
W. 24cm.
M.77-1947

(b) Design, a frieze of dogs and putti
Etching by Stefano della Bella (1610-64)
Lettered; 'stef. Del. Bella Inu. & Fec. Cum Priuil Regis 12'
8.3 × 24.8cm.
28190.9

By the end of the 17th century, Benjamin Pyne was in the
front rank of goldsmiths who, along with Anthony Nelme,
shared the main responsibility of upholding native standards
against Huguenot competition. In 1697, Pyne was one of the
signatories to a petition submitted to the Goldsmiths'
Company protesting about foreign goldsmiths settling in
London, but he nonetheless, like Nelme, probably employed
Huguenot journeymen in his workshop. In 1725, he was
elected Prime Warden of the Goldsmiths' Company but
poverty forced him to resign from the Livery only two years
later, and he died destitute in 1732.
The design of the chasing on the border is based on that of an
etched frieze by Stefano della Bella. He was a Florentine who
produced over 1,400 engravings in a career which took him to
Paris (1639-50) and Rome where he was principally under the
influence of the Medici. His 82-odd plates of engraved
ornament were particularly influential and were frequently
reprinted; individual motifs were borrowed and used in a
variety of different media up until the late 18th century (see
also plate 20).

arrive in some numbers during the Commonwealth, and
increased immediately before and after the persecution of
Protestants in France. Louis XIV held fundamental
objections to the Calvinist doctrines of the Huguenot
population, suspecting that they also cultivated republi-
can tendencies. In 1685 the French King revoked the
Edict of Nantes, which since 1598 had guaranteed the
civil and religious liberties of the Huguenot population,
presenting the Protestants with two bald alternatives;
either to convert to Catholicism or to leave. Most of them
left and ultimately over a quarter of a million skilled arti-
sans and merchants emigrated to the Low Countries,
England and other Protestant countries. The replacement of James II, who had sought to re-establish Catholicism in England, by the Protestant Dutch prince,
William of Orange in the 'Glorious Revolution' of 1688,
further enhanced the status of England as a Protestant

refuge. William III's own court architect and designer,
Daniel Marot, was a French refugee who had entered the
King's service after the Revocation of the Edict of
Nantes, and thus the accession of William of Orange,
although Dutch himself, had the anomalous effect of
encouraging French fashions in England.

Apart from Court taste, the public were growing
weary of the lavish, embossed ornament of the Carolean
goldsmiths, and were beginning to favour more simpli-
fied forms, but at the same time demanded greater virtu-
osity in the detailing. The Carolean technique had its
limitations; although it was effective when viewed from a
distance, close inspection revealed these. The metal was
necessarily thin, so that it could be easily stretched for
embossing, which gave the object an insubstantial and
fragile appearance; but it was in the production of cast
detail in particular where the English goldsmiths, before
the main Huguenot arrival, were at their weakest.

Casting was normally used for the production of
external details requiring strength such as spouts, handles
and the feet of an object. A pattern or former would be
carefully modelled, often in wood or metal in the 17th
century, and pressed into a sand mould (the 'marl')
strengthened with additives so that a crisp impression was
made. Two impressions would be made of each half of the
feature to be modelled, and the pattern was then
removed; the two sand moulds were clamped together
and molten metal poured in through a gate at the top.
Subsequently any excess material was removed by chasing. The molten metal had to be of good quality and the
correct temperature scrupulously observed in order to
avoid pitting and firestain. This technicality was not
always fully appreciated by the Carolean goldsmiths, but
it was in the final chasing where they proved to be particularly inept. The results were decidedly crude in
comparison with their French counterparts and thus the
Huguenots were well equipped to satisfy the increasing
public demand for finely executed cast ornament.
Within a short time of their arrival they were being
awarded the majority of the important commissions for
new plate in London.

Understandably, this incensed the English goldsmiths
who made several attempts to prevent the Huguenots
from practising their trade. It is not difficult to appreciate
why the less able goldsmiths were sensitive to this sudden
influx of competition from the Continent. Not only
were they able to provide new fashions in silver which
were beginning to be accepted enthusiastically by the
more discerning members of the public, but also because
of their impoverished condition on arrival in England,
they were prepared to work for lower rates.

9

8
(a) Ewer
Silver gilt
Hallmarks for London 1700-01;
maker's mark of David Willaume
Engraved with the arms of Hill of
Hawstone, Shropshire
Bond Collection
H. 21cm. W. 15cm.
822-1890
The arms are probably those of the
Hon. Rev. Richard Hill (1655-1727), a
distinguished statesman and diplomat
of Queen Anne's reign.

(b) Ewer
Silver
Hallmarks for London 1714-15;
maker's mark of Pierre Platel
Engraved with the arms of Temple
Bequeathed by Major Thomas Sutton
Timmis
H. 23cm. W. 16.5cms.
M.71-1933
David Willaume was born in Metz
and was probably trained either by his
father or another Metz goldsmith. It is
not recorded when he arrived in
England but he took out denization
papers on December 16, 1687, was
made a Freeman of the Goldsmiths'
Company in c 1693, and a Liveryman
in October 1698.
He enjoyed the patronage of some of
the wealthiest clients in England from
the latter part of the reign of William
III to the end of George I's. All his
surviving work displays the highest
qualities of design and execution.
Pierre Platel was born in Lille, c 1664.
His father fled with his family to
Flanders in 1685. Pierre Platel, and his
brother Claude arrived in England in
1688, shortly after the accession of
William III. He was made a Freeman
of the Company in June 1699 and died
on May 21, 1719.
Like Willaume, he was one of the
most successful Huguenot silversmiths working in London.
The helmet shaped ewer was a type
introduced by Huguenot silversmiths
and became standard for as long as
ewers remained popular. The
combination of cut card work and
applied cast straps gave tremendous
scope for rich plastic ornamentation.

9 (*opposite*)
(a) Teapot with stand and lamp
Silver
Hallmarks for London 1705-06;
maker's mark of Simon Pantin
Engraved with an unidentified coat of
arms
Harvey Haddon Gift
H. 20.5cms.
M.172-b-1919

(b) Chocolate pot
Silver
Hallmarks for London 1704-05;
maker's mark of William Fawdrey
T.H. Cobb Bequest
H. 27.5cms.
M.1819-1944

(c) Candlestick
Silver
Hallmarks for London 1711-12;
maker's mark of Pierre Platel
Engraved with the arms of Goodwin
H. 16cms. W. 10cms.
M.850-1926

Simon Pantin came from a Rouen
family of goldsmiths. He was apprenticed to Pierre Harrache and made a
Freeman of the Company on June 4th,
1701. He had a considerable output
and specialized in the production of
high quality domestic plate.
William Fawdrey was an English
goldsmith, the son of an Oxford
family. He was apprenticed to Robert
Cooper in 1683 and gained his freedom in August 1694. He was the sig-
natory to several petitions protesting
about the marking of foreigners' plate
and the granting of the Company's
Freedom to Huguenot silversmiths
resident in London. Nonetheless, the
accomplished use of cut card work on
the chocolate pot illustrated suggests
that he was perfectly willing to
employ Huguenot journeymen in his
own workshop.

10
Two handled cup and cover
Silver
No hallmarks; maker's mark for George
Wickes on cup only, used 1722-35 (see
Grimwade No 9183)
Cancellation of transposed marks by
Goldsmiths Hall, No 4580, effected 1975
Dated c 1735
H. 30.5cm. W. 34.5cm.
M.280 and a-1975
This 101 oz cup and cover is applied with
cast and chased vine decoration and
engraved with the triumph of Bacchus
beneath the rim. The engraved armorials
are those of the Hon John Scrope (Azure
a bend or) who is known from the
Garrard Ledgers to have been a client of
George Wickes. The cup is a duty-
dodger; its marks have been transposed by
Wickes from an earlier piece of plate to

avoid the excise duty of 6d per ounce pay-
able on assay. Its appearance in the ledgers
would have been incriminating for both
patron and goldsmith; each saves the large
sum of £2.10s in duty by this not
uncommon deception.
The dating of unmarked pieces depends
on their style; the asymmetry of the
applied scrollwork suggests the earlier
phase of the rococo, while the handle
pattern is known to have been used by
other silversmiths – Paul Crespin, John le
Sage and Paul de Lamerie among them –
between 1732 and 1743.

Caster and three tea caddies

(a) Caster, silver, hallmarks for London 1734-5; maker's mark of Paul de Lamerie

H. 16cm. Diam. 7.6cm.

M.157-1939

One of de Lamerie's last attempts in the French 'Regence' manner before he turned to rococo design.

(b) Tea caddy, silvergilt, no hallmarks, but attributed to de Lamerie. Engraved with the arms of Antonio Lopez Suasso impaling Da Costa, probably by William Hogarth, c 1720 (Folio 18, *Hogarth Engravings*, Brit. Lib.)

H. 12.4cms. W. 7.6cms.

M.314-1962

(c) Tea caddy, silver, hallmarks for London 1735-6; maker's mark of Paul de Lamerie

Engraved with arms of Knipe

H. 14cms. W. 8cms.

M. 156-1939

(d) Tea caddy, silvergilt hallmarks for London 1741-2; maker's mark of Paul de Lamerie

H. 12.7cms. W. 9.9cms.

M.49-1940

Paul de Lamerie was a second generation Huguenot. Apprenticed to Pierre Platel, (see plates 8 & 9) he worked in all styles fashionable throughout his long career from 1712 to 1751; but he is chiefly remembered for being one of the first and most proficient silversmiths to work in the rococo manner.

Two petitions, in 1682 and 1683, were placed before the court of the Goldsmiths' Company protesting about the admission of Huguenots to the Company's freedom. The English craftsmen had been partially successful at invoking an ancient clause in the Goldsmiths' charter which permitted only freemen of the Company to have their wares assayed at Goldsmiths' Hall. At the same time, another clause in the Company's charter forbade unmarked wares from being sold within the City boundaries. The immigrant goldsmiths were placed in a very difficult position. Some were lucky enough to gain a royal appointment which automatically removed any obligation to become a member of the city guild. A few distinguished Huguenot goldsmiths were granted the freedom of the Company soon after their arrival; for example, Pierre Harache in July 1682, and incidentally one of the most gifted amongst them. But the accompanying protests which invariably greeted such exceptions forced the wardens to tread warily. Others were content to remain journeymen, working for English goldsmiths and abandoning any ambition of establishing themselves in their own business. This no doubt helped to disseminate French fashions throughout the trade and break down the rivalry between the foreigners and the English goldsmiths. Ultimately, in 1725, their exclusion from full membership of the Goldsmiths' Company was ruled to be illegal but by then the issue was academic for

11

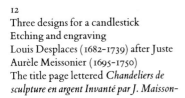

12
Three designs for a candlestick
Etching and engraving
Louis Desplaces (1682-1739) after Juste
Aurèle Meissonier (1695-1750)
The title page lettered *Chandeliers de
sculpture en argent Invanté par J. Maisson-*

nier Architecte en 1728. Desplaces Sculpsit.
The plates lettered *Meissonier Architecte in
Desplaces Sculpsit. Avec Privilège du Roi.*
One also lettered with the address of
Huquier
27 × 21cms; 26.9 × 21cms; 26.9 × 21.2cms;
27988 CI; E.1663 and A-1977

The severe asymmetry of Meissonier's
candlestick of 1728 required three views in
order to show the design of the whole. It
is one of the earliest examples of 'rocaille'
which was one of the principal
components of the mid-eighteenth-
century rococo style.

the Huguenots had fully succeeded in integrating themselves into the London community.

After the accession of William and Mary, the tensions
within the trade were eased by a general increase in prosperity and the consequent rise in the demand for new
plate. This overall expansion of the goldsmiths' trade put
considerable strain on the available resources of bullion.
Unlike his counterpart in the reign of Elizabeth I, when
new sources of supply were opened up in the Americas,
the late-17th-century goldsmith was faced with a static
supply. The inevitable consequences were that a considerable amount of existing plate was consigned to the
melting pot, and this accounts further for the scarcity of
extant pieces dating from before this time. Moreover the
goldsmiths resorted to melting the coinage, since it was
minted to the same sterling standard as wrought silver, or
alternatively to clipping the edges of coins.

The continued withdrawal of coinage was damaging
to the country's economy and accordingly, in 1697, new
coins with milled edges were issued, and the standard of
purity for wrought plate was increased from the sterling
standard of 11 oz 2 dwt per Troy pound to 11 oz 10 dwt. To
signify this change the hallmarks were replaced by a lion's
head erased and the seated figure of Britannia. This new
standard henceforth became known as the Britannia

standard. In addition the makers' marks were changed.
The new legislation required that instead of the maker's
initials, or sometimes a simple device, the new mark was
to be made up of the first two letters of the maker's sur-
name. This system was mandatory until 1719 when the
Wrought Plate Act re-introduced the sterling standard,
which from then on was generally adopted. The Britannia standard however remained optional. It was, and still
is, sometimes used by silversmiths of whom the Huguenot Paul de Lamerie was one. Although its greater purity
made the cost of the metal more expensive, its greater
refinement made it more ductile and therefore more suit-
able for casting.

Thus the arrival of the Huguenots had a decisive effect
both on the administration of the trade itself, and on the
stylistic requirements of the public at large. Their virtu-
osity with cast work has already been discussed. Another
technique in which they excelled was in their use of cut
card work which, although occasionally used by English
goldsmiths before the Huguenot arrival, was most successfully exploited by the Huguenots themselves. Cut
card work means the soldering of thin perforated sheets
of silver onto plain surfaces. Often a foliate pattern was
adopted and the ornament was usually applied to the
junction of the foot and base of a vessel, or the uppermost

13
(a) Apollo and Daphne Candlesticks
(Two of a set of four)
Silver
No hallmarks but probably London,
c 1740-45
After a design by George Michael
Moser RA (1706-83)
H. 37 cm. W. 17cm.
M.329-c-1977

(b) Design for a candlestick
Pen, ink and wash
Signed G.M. Moser iv & delt.
35 × 20cm.
E.4895-1968

One of Moser's sources for this design is undoubtedly the marble group in the Galleria Borghese, Rome, of Apollo and Daphne by Bernini in 1625. The story of Apollo's pursuit of Daphne and her transformation into a laurel tree on the point of capture, symbolic of the victory of Chastity over Love, had for long been a popular subject with artists. The rococo elements in the design are the violent twist to the figure of Daphne, the replacement of the bark by soft drapery, the treatment of the base and the transformation of the look on Daphne's face from one of terror to one of almost supreme complacency.

These candlesticks could have been made by any one of the leading silver-smiths of the 1740s such as Wickes, Shruder, de Lamerie or Crespin and are intended to be seen from two different view points. One is as illustrated, corresponding to Bernini's grouping. The alternative is with the cartouches on the bases facing forward so that the figures appear to be running towards the viewer, giving sideways glances to each other; as if following the actor's convention that they must always face the audience, regardless of their relationship to each other.

14
Coffee-pot
Silver
Hallmarks for London 1749-50,
maker's mark of James Shruder
(active 1737-1749)
Engraved with the armorials of
Okeover impaling Nichol for Leake
Okeover (1701-65), and his wife,
Mary Nichol
H. 28.3cm. W. 26cm.
M.312-1975
The design of the cast spout is almost
certainly drawn from the title page of
Jacques de Lajoue's second *Livre de
Cartouches* (published in Paris c 1734).

15
The Ashburnham centrepiece (in the
form of a tureen on a stand)
Silver
Hallmarks for London 1747-8;
maker's mark of Nicholas Sprimont
(1716-70).
Cast and mantled armorials of John,
2nd Earl of Ashburnham (1724-1812),
and those of his wife Elizabeth
Crowley whom he married in 1756.
L. 60.8cm. H. 46.5cm.
M.46-1971
Sprimont was born in Liege on the
23rd of January 1716 and later
apprenticed to his uncle and god-
father, Nicholas Joseph Sprimont. He
probably arrived in England early in
1742 as he was married in Knights-
bridge chapel later that same year.
Surviving examples of his silverwork
are extremely rare and all date from
between 1742 and 1747. He may well
have collaborated on a number of
pieces with Paul Crespin; they both
had workshops in Compton Street,
Soho. Towards the end of the 1740s,
he abandoned silversmithing to
become head of the Chelsea Porcelain
Factory. The Ashburnham centrepiece is one of his largest pieces
executed in silver and anticipates some
of his later work in porcelain.

surface of the cover of a cup. At first single and integral sheets of silver were used, but the Huguenots soon learnt to vary this by applying foliate detail in separate leaves or adjusting the depth of the pattern by varying the thickness of the cut sheet and sometimes applying cast mouldings to it. Great care was needed since the goldsmith had to contend with solder flowing at different rates.

The combination of cast work and cut card work produced, in the hands of the Huguenot silversmiths, a rich plastic ornamentation executed with classical formality. The anti-classical nature of Carolean ornament with its exotic naturalism and grotesque element was completely rejected. The desire for a formal ornamental language, after a period dominated by a picturesque language using natural, realistic and exotic forms, will be seen as a recurring feature throughout this study.

Not all silver produced after the Huguenot arrival was necessarily richly embellished. Not all the English goldsmiths had the technical proficiency or the clientele to support the Huguenot taste. Thus a fashion for silver of extreme sobriety emerged, which was virtually devoid of ornament and relied for its aesthetic appeal on excellent proportions, contrasting plain surfaces and a restrained use of stepped mouldings. It has been popularly named the 'Queen Anne' style although it was current well beyond the brief period of her reign. It has been sometimes argued that this fashion is wholly English in origin, occurring and flourishing independently of Huguenot influence, but it is doubtful whether this is true. The quality of craftsmanship which was noticeably superior to that of the Carolean goldsmiths, and the carefully judged proportions of the designs were undoubtedly the result of Huguenot influence. By the 1730s the two styles had merged. English and Huguenot goldsmiths' work had become virtually indistinguishable from each other, but the characteristics of the Huguenot manner remained dominant. A baroque classicism had become very much the established taste, and new influences were beginning to emerge. For the next thirty years, silversmiths executed work in the rococo style.

This was again a fashion imported from France. The name is derived from the character of the ornament which is such a feature of this style; rocaille or rockwork, which reflects a return to an interest in the grotesque and the introduction of naturalistic elements. The most sophisticated exponent was the Turin born architect, Juste-Aurele Meissonier, who was appointed designer to the French Court in 1724 and admitted to the Paris guild of goldsmiths the following year by the highly unusual means of a royal 'lettre de cachet'. In 1734 he began to issue a series of drawings executed in the course of his royal duties and for commissions undertaken by private patrons. Shortly afterwards they were collected by Huquier and published in one volume titled *Oeuvre de Juste Aurele Messonier peintre, sculpteur architect et dessinateur de la Chambre et cabinet du Roy*. By then the fashion itself was fully established in both England and France. Huquier's publication is important, not because it introduced the style to England, although it was no doubt immensely influential once it became available, but because by containing drawings of Meissonier's work over several years, it exhibits the development of this style and all its essential features.

One of the most dominant characteristics of Meissonier's work was the severe asymmetrical quality of the design; for example, a design for a silver candlestick for Louis XV dated 1728 (see plate 12) where three different engravings were necessary, representing different viewpoints, to convey properly the three-dimensional quality of the design. This structural irregularity was a new departure although Van Vianen had earlier used asymmetrical surface detail. The rich scrollwork however was ultimately derived from the 16th-century Italian interest in irregular rockwork and shellwork formations which initially graced the designs of garden grottoes and eventually came to form an ornamental language in its own right. Naturalistic imagery was an important feature of the rococo style. Even the design for the base of this candlestick, although highly abstract in treatment, is reminiscent of a cascade of falling water, swirling and forming eddies as it tumbles into a pool. But naturalistic imagery not only influenced the basic conception of the design for a piece of silver but also was used more obviously for providing ornamental detail. Animal, vegetable and mineral subjects were grouped in fantastic juxtapositions, often ignoring conventional proportions (see plate 15). It was this last characteristic, giving many pieces an air of whimsical unreality, which was to draw much criticism in later years once the taste for the rococo had waned.

Thus we have the essential elements of the rococo style; a richness of detail combined with an irregularity of form, which were dependent on an interest in organic naturalism. It was first introduced to England by Hubert Francois Gravelot who arrived in London in 1732. He is best known as an illustrator and decorator of books, but to his contemporaries he was equally well known as a teacher of design. Gravelot established his own drawing school off the Strand and, after 1745, was one of the luminaries of the St. Martin's Lane Academy, a drawing school founded by William Hogarth ten years earlier when he acquired the collection of casts of his father-in-law, Sir James Thornhill.

George Vertue, the engraver and antiquary, has by his invaluable notebooks left us one of the few documented contemporary accounts of the artistic influences operating within the decorative arts in the middle of the 18th century. He states clearly that Gravelot designed for silversmiths, joiners and cabinet makers, and in his published designs showed that 'he is endowed with a great and fruitful genius for designs, inventions of history and ornaments'. The novelty of Gravelot's designs can be attributed to their rococo character, directly imported from France, and immensely influential; for it was shortly after his arrival that the silversmiths such as Paul de Lamerie and George Wickes began to experiment in the rococo style.

Unfortunately, the pattern books used by Gravelot to teach rococo ornament and composition have disappeared, and it is therefore difficult to assess his own contribution to English silver design and the exact degree to which other English silversmiths themselves adapted his ideas. We are a little more fortunate in the case of George Michael Moser, a Swiss who emigrated to London in 1721. Moser's fame nowadays chiefly rests on his reputation as a highly skilled chaser of objects of vertu. He was equally important as a teacher of rococo ornament and design. Like Gravelot he established his own school and again was one of the prominent members of Hogarth's Academy.

16
Condiment set
Silver
Hallmarks for London 1758-9; maker's mark of Arthur Annesley
H. 13cm W. 14cms. (centre vessel)
M.26-b-1982
This set is closely related to a contemporary design by John Linnell (1729-96)

Teaching was carried out by example and imitation, and imported pattern books from France were important educational tools. The engravings of designers such as Jacques de Lajoue, Gaetano Brunetti and Pierre Germain, who in 1748 published his *Elements d'Orfèverie*, were widely circulated. Students seem to have been actively encouraged to interpret designs with a certain freedom though adhering to theoretical principles which were later expounded by Hogarth in his *Analysis of Beauty*, published in 1754. This is illustrated by comparing a candlestick design by Moser with a contemporary version in silver by an unidentified silversmith (although probably chased by Moser himself) (see plate 13a). The caryatid form was a favourite baroque device, while the rococo element in the design is the violent twist to the figure of Daphne, the soft and enveloping drapery, and the rocaille decoration of the base. The silversmith has introduced his own variations, treating the base more naturalistically and reducing the drapery to give a crisper outline to the figure.

The silversmiths who dominated the 1740s were Paul Crespin, Nicholas Sprimont (see plate 15) and Paul de Lamerie (see plate 11) who were all Huguenots, although there were notable exceptions such as the German James Shruder (see plate 14) and the Englishman George Wickes. By the 1750s the rococo taste was firmly established, and the majority of London silver workshops produced goods in the rococo manner. In the hands of less adventurous goldsmiths, designs were often standardised and repetitious, but the level of technical execution remained consistently high. Embossed work became extremely popular, incorporating chinoiserie and floral decoration which had re-emerged as favourite motifs

(see plate 17). Later in the 1760s openwork became increasingly popular, heralding neo-classicism. An increasing lightness of effect is evident, exemplified by the ingenious wire decoration on the covers of the condiment jars in plate 16.

By the 1770s the rococo had run its course and had ceased to be the dominant decorative language amongst fashionable silversmiths. The cool, restrained qualities inherent in the neo-classical style which replaced it were the very antithesis of the frivolity and licentiousness of the rococo. But neo-classicism was not merely a reaction to an established taste. Its sources were very much more diverse.

One of the many intellectual achievements of the 18th century was the emergence of materialist individualism; that man was the arbiter and master of his own fate rather than the victim of pre-ordained destiny. The ideas expressed by such writers as Voltaire, Montesquieu and Diderot, for example, sought to liberate society from its established pessimism and superstition, and create a climate of optimism which encouraged progressive social and moral improvement. Thus the traditional philosophical values endorsed by the Church and the classics — long accepted but hitherto never seriously questioned — underwent a thorough reappraisal and it was inevitable that aesthetic values came to be included in the philosophical debate. The taste for neo-classicism, which had inspired designers in different ways for centuries, was not merely a revival of antique forms. A return to first principles was also being sought.

European aristocratic society in the 18th century enjoyed an unusual cultural homogeneity, not equalled before or since, which encouraged the broad dissemination of these new ideas. Manners and social behaviour, as much as intellectual debate tended to copy those of the French Court; and the 'Grand Tour' of Europe, regarded by the 18th century gentleman as an essential part of his education, included obligatory stops in Paris and Rome.

Italy exerted a unique attraction and influence. Rome was the centre of Christendom, and the inspiration behind a gentleman's classical education. It was also the centre of archaeological excavation for antiquities, though important finds were also being made elsewhere. In 1738 Charles, the Bourbon King of Naples, instigated

17

17
Three tea caddies
Silver
(a) Hallmarks for London 1766-7; maker's mark: ER
H. 13.3cms. W. 9cms.
M.1770-1944

(b) Hallmarks for 1766-7, maker's mark of Samuel Taylor
H. 14cms. W. 9.5cms.
M.1771-1944

(c) Hallmarks for 1763-4; maker's mark of Edward Aldridge
Engraved with unidentified arms and crest
H. 13cms. W. 8cms.
M.1769-1944
W.J. Johnson Bequest

18
Sauceboat and cover (one of a set of
eight)
Silver
Hallmarks for Birmingham 1776–7;
maker's mark of Matthew
Boulton and John Fothergill
Designed by Robert Adam
L. 25cms. H. 13cms. D. 11.8cms.
Circ.513-1953
One of the most successful Adam
designs produced by Matthew
Boulton in the early years of his Soho
Foundry Birmingham.

19
(a) Vase and cover
Silver
Hallmark for London 1771-2; maker's
mark of Charles Wright
H. 38cms. Diam. 15cms.
751-1877

(b) Coffee pot
Silver
Hallmark for London 1776-7; maker's
mark of Charles Wright
H. 34.6cms. Diam. 13cms.
752-1877

excavations at Herculaneum, which were suspended in 1740, but resumed with renewed vigour in 1745 and finally terminated in 1765. At Pompeii, excavations began in 1748 and immediately produced astonishing finds.

Up until the middle of the 18th century these discoveries were mostly fortuitous and largely due to private initiative. Gradually, as a result of the increasing interest and trading in antiquities, excavations became more systematic. The excavations at Herculaneum under state patronage were an example of an increasing professional attitude to archaeology. In Rome, Winckelmann, the German scholar and advisor to Cardinal Albani, was appointed Commissioner of Antiquities in 1764. He, through the publication of his book, *History of Ancient Art,* did more than any other single scholar to propagate the virtues of Greek Art. In his official capacity, he introduced a licensing system which ensured that a proportion of antiquities discovered were reserved for the State while the remainder passed into private hands. This policy encouraged the foundation of some of the major English collections of antiquities including one of the greatest of them all; that of Sir William Hamilton. It was d'Harcanville's introduction and catalogue to Hamilton's collection published in 1776-7 (amongst other influential publications such as the *Receuil d'Antiquities,* (1752-1767) by the Comte de Caylus, the architectural studies of Wood and Dawkins *The Ruins of Palmyra* 1753, Piranesi's *Della Magnificanza ed Architettura dei Romani* (1761), Robert Adam's study of the ruins of Diocletian's palace in Spalato, (started in 1754) and later, Stuart and Revett's *Antiquities of Athens* (1788)) which were to prove invaluable sources of inspiration for English silversmiths.

Robert Adam (1728-92), along with his brother James, was primarily responsible for popularising the neo-classical style in Britain and it is for this reason that the years 1760-1800, in the history of English silversmithing, are traditionally referred to as the 'Adam' period. However, their influence on silversmithing was chiefly indirect and exercised through their architectural work and archaeological publications. Robert Adam did produce a number of designs for plate for clients whose houses he had built, although few of these were ever actually executed. Matthew Boulton did produce a sauceboat to one of Robert Adam's designs (see plate 18) which proved very successful and a partnership at one stage was proposed between Adam and Boulton but this failed to materialise.

The success of English neo-classical silver was achieved by a harmonious balancing of form and ornament. For holloware, the form of the Greek vase proved very adaptable and immensely popular. Such articles as covered cups, teapots and candlesticks required rather more ingenuity and often relied more on their applied decoration, such as floral swags, or draped linen between symmetrically placed rosettes, and a variety of raised acanthus leaves for their neo-classical content. Such devices were freely and often successfully used for silverwork although they mainly originated from architectural or ceramic sources. One of the peculiarities of the neo-classical silversmith was that his knowledge of classical art was derived from every medium but his own. The large hoards of Roman plate were not discovered until the 19th century: that of Bernay in 1830, Hildesheim in 1868 and Boscoreau in 1895. However, archaeological exactitude was not the dominant concern of the silversmith in the late 18th century. The Antique was seen as a model for the artist's own inspiration. Winkelmann declared 'There is only one way for the moderns to become great and perhaps unequalled: by imitating the Ancients' and qualified this by saying 'the opposite of independent thought is for me the copy, not the imitation'. Antiquity was to be imitated; it was not to be copied. The essential qualities of the silversmith's work were regular proportions and symmetrically applied ornament, which correlated with the contemporary interpretation of Graeco-Roman art.

Up until the late 18th century, London was the leading British centre of plate manufacture but improvement in manufacturing techniques, particularly in the provincial centres of Birmingham and Sheffield, were steadily eroding the capital's pre-eminence. The rolling mill, which produced sheets of metal of a uniform thickness, had already been in use for at least half a century but more recent innovations included the fly press, which permitted accurate and repetitive piercing, a machine patented in 1779 for making beaded wires, and new steel alloys of greater durability which improved the accuracy and complexity of die stamping.

This increasing mechanisation encouraged new working methods in the larger provincial factories, and piece work became generally accepted. This was already well established in the Birmingham gunmaking industry and the more enterprising silversmiths, such as Matthew Boulton, shrewdly appreciated its advantages. The process of manufacture was divided amongst several workers, each repetitively producing the same elements which, along with mechanical aids, required less skill on their part and greatly increased the speed of production. This had two immediate effects. Mechanical production favoured the design of objects having a simple structure, with easily repeated ornament, and therefore tended to be restricted to small items of domestic plate. This then created a new market, for mechanisation also reduced the cost of plate which meant it could now be bought by a public which had hitherto been unable to contemplate it. The consumption of plate expanded at a noticeably greater rate than the increase in population, and the flood of mechanised wares from Birmingham and Sheffield challenged the techniques and assumptions of the more conservative London goldsmiths. Nonetheless, the latter successfully dominated the market in commissioned

pieces which required superior design and execution, only achieved by individual craftsmanship.

But the distinctions were eroding. The Sheffield manufacturers could produce candlesticks that could compete, in every respect, very favourably on the London market, and were becoming extremely exercised by the practice of some London silversmiths who over-

20
(a) Chocolate pot
Silver
Hallmarks for London 1777-8; maker's mark of Henry Greenway
H.32.7 cm. Diam. 14 cm.
460-1875

(b) Vase
Silver
Hallmarks for London 1770-71; maker's mark of John Parker and Edward Wakelin.
H. 21.3cm. W. 8.6cm.
564-1874

(c) Candlestick
Silver
Hallmarks for Sheffield 1774-5; maker's mark of George Ashforth & Co.
H. 29.2cm. W. 13cm.
832-1890
The design of this vase initially appears in a series of etchings by Stefano della Bella (*Raccolta di Vasi diversi*, pl. 6, VAM 2974 A6) which were issued between 1639 and 1648, and was subsequently reworked by Robert Adam. They were frequently referred to during the period of English 'vase mania' after 1770. Adam's design is included amongst his drawings in the Sir John Soames' Museum (*Adam Drawings* Vol. 25, no. 157).

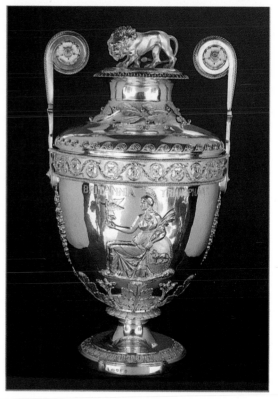

21
Sugar basin
Silvergilt, set with medallions after James Tassie
Hallmarks for London 1777-8; maker's mark of Andrew
Fogelberg
H. 9.2cm. Diam. 8cm.
M.295-1962
Two of the medallions are no's 6331 and 6332 in the 1791 Tassie
catalogue. The third has not been identified.

Teapot and stand
Silvergilt
Hallmarks for London 1784-5, maker's mark of Andrew
Fogelberg and Stephen Gilbert
H. 14cm. L. 26cm.
M.47 and a-1860
There is no record of Fogelberg ever serving his apprenticeship in London. His name suggests a Swedish origin and it is
possible that he emigrated to this country already trained as a
goldsmith. He was in partnership with Stephen Gilbert from
1780 to 1793, after which he continued working alone until
c 1800.
His work, whether in partnership or alone, displays an elegant
restrained classicism, particularly in his speciality of using
small cast cameo medallions based on Tassie's paste gems
which were popular in England at the time.

22
The Trafalgar vase
Silver
Hallmarks for London 1805-06; maker's mark of Digby Scott
and Benjamin Smith
Designed by John Flaxman RA (1755-1826)
Inscribed: 'BRITONS STRIKE HOME/BRITANNIA TRIUMPHANT'

Bond Gift
H. 43cms. W. 25.7cms.
803-1890
Commissioned by Lloyd's Patriotic Fund for presentation to
surviving senior officers of the Battle of Trafalgar

23
Teapot and hot water jug on stands
Silver gilt
Hallmarks for London 1804-05; maker's mark of Paul Storr
for Rundell Bridge and Rundell, and on spirit burners of
Digby Scott and Benjamin Smith.
 Engraved crests of Vane for William Harry Vane, 3rd Earl of
Darlington KG (1766-1842), later Marquess of Cleveland
(1827), Baron Raby and Duke of Cleveland (1833)
H. 26.5cms. W. 16cms. (hot water jug)
Lent by V. Morley Lawson
This matching pair of vessels was made to complement a
similarly ornamented kettle shaped tea urn, also by Storr, of
1802-03. The distinctive form of the hot water jug was
employed by Storr from c 1803 to after 1810; most examples
having a tripod stand.

on the outskirts of Birmingham. At one time he had over
a thousand workmen employed there. Boulton was personally acquainted with many of the leading English
architects and designers who had visited Italy: a cultivated man who acquainted himself with all the latest
archaeological and architectural publications, he produced goods of a consistently high quality. He is perhaps
chiefly remembered nowadays for his collaboration with
James Watt in the development and promotion of a commercial steam engine. Equally significant was his successful campaign to establish a Birmingham Assay Office.

By 1800, the taste for silver in the Adam style was
beginning to decline. Increasing criticism was being
made of its flimsy and insubstantial appearance. This was
endorsed by the architect, Charles Heathcote Tatham
(1772-1842) who, in 1799, published *Ancient Ornamental
Architecture at Rome and in Italy* and in 1806 his influential
Designs for Ornamental Plate where he complained that
'instead of Massiveness, the principle characteristic of
good plate, light and insignificant forms have prevailed,
to the utter exclusion of all good ornament whatever'.
Tatham's stress on attention to ornament and quality of
finish was heeded widely by manufacturers. The political

stamped the Sheffield makers' mark with that of their
own and sold them for a handsome profit. The Birmingham firm of Matthew Boulton, in particular, could
compete with the London market on equal terms. Boulton was the epitome of the successful entrepreneur. He
rapidly assimilated new ideas and inventions, successfully putting them into practice in his new Soho foundry

24
(a) Wine Cooler
Silvergilt
Hallmarks for 1809; maker's mark of Paul Storr at the Dean Street workshop of Rundell, Bridge and Rundell
H. 35cm. W. 26.5cm.
ex. Ormonde Collection
M.48 and a-1982

(b) Design for a wine cooler
Pen drawing, after William Theed.
26.7 × 24.7cm.
D.378-1886.
The relief represents the triumph of Bacchus with a staggering Silenus bringing up the rear.
The original model of this piece was probably by William Theed, and based on a vase in the Villa Albani, engraved by C.H. Tatham in *Etchings, Representing the Best Examples of Ancient Ornamental Architecture*. (1799; pl. 28).
The design (showing the opposite side of the vase) was one which was reproduced many times by both Benjamin Smith and Paul Storr. While the body remained unchanged, the base was adapted to suit the purse of the customer. The design shows a cheaper version than that supplied to the Marquess of Ormonde who in turn had a less elaborate example than those supplied for the Royal Collections.

upheavals at the time ironically contributed to the desire for monumentality in plate design. Napoleon's expeditions in Egypt (1798) caught the imagination of Europe. Baron Denon's published account of his journey up the Nile in 1802 was an instant success in London and did much to acquaint the public with Egyptian culture and iconography. Sir Arthur Wellesley's campaigns in India also provided suitably exotic subject matter. Military ventures often provided serving officers with tremendous opportunity for financial gain. Evidence of this is the large presentation of plate of 1803 to Sir Arthur (later Duke of Wellington) by officers under his command in the Deccan.

During this period, despite the political turmoil of the Napoleonic Wars, goldsmiths were not short of work. Presentations of plate to national heroes became an increasingly popular practice. Lloyd's Patriotic Fund, a consortium of merchants and bankers from the City of London, commissioned the sculptor John Flaxman to design a vase of which some sixty-six copies were made and mainly presented to the senior naval officers who had taken part in the Battle of Trafalgar (see plate 22). Moreover, the Prince of Wales, who became Prince Regent in 1811 and in 1820 George IV, stimulated the production of ceremonial plate by his extravagant and regular orders

for several elaborate services. It was his extensive patronage that has given rise to the term 'Regency', used to
describe this period in the history of English silver.

Flaxman's design for the Trafalgar vase is in the neo-
classical manner which was still the prevailing taste. But
the early-19th-century neo-classicism differed substantially from that of the previous generation. Tatham's
strictures on his perceived deficiencies of the 'Adam' style
were widely noted. Silversmiths turned their attention to
the florid opulence of Imperial Rome for inspiration and
eschewed the relative primitivism of early Greek Art.
The intellectual vigour of the neo-classical movement
which had sought to substantiate an art with values of
eternal validity had been largely dissipated, and attention
to the antique concentrated on mere historicism. It
became increasingly a revivalist exercise with greater

25
Sugar bowl
Silver gilt
Hallmarks for London 1805-06; maker's mark of Digby Scott
and Bejamin Smith
Given in memory of Alexander Alan Paton CBE by his sister
Mary Paton
H. 17cm. W. 19cm.
M.597.1936

Candlestick
Silver gilt
Hallmarks for London 1814.15; maker's mark of Paul Storr
Engraved with the cypher A.M. below a coronet. Said to have
belonged to a Duke of Cumberland, probably Ernest
Augustus (1771-1851) son of George III, who became King
Ernest of Hanover in 1837
Given by Mr L.A. Crichton
H. 22.5cm. W. 14cm.
M.57 and a-1925
Both pieces were made on behalf of the Royal Goldsmiths and
bear the Latin inscription round each base:
'RUNDELL BRIDGE ET RUNDELL AURIFICES REGIS ET PRINCIPIS
WALLIAE REGENTIS BRITANNIAS' (Rundell and Bridge and
Rundell, goldsmiths to the King and the Prince of Wales,
Regent of Britain).

26
Design for a standing cup and cover
Pencil and wash
John Flaxman RA
Inscribed in ink: 'cup designed for George IV, St. George
St. Andrew St. Patrick by J. Flaxman'.
32.5 × 10.5cm.
D.379-1886
The cup which was executed from this design in 1824 by John
Bridge is known as 'The National Cup' and is part of the
Royal Plate at Windsor Castle.

27
(a) Vase and cover
Silver gilt
Hallmarks for London 1827-8; maker's mark of Rebecca Emes
and Edward Barnard
Inscribed: 'WEYMOUTH REGATTA 1827'
Bond Collection
H. 38.5cm. W. 23.5cm.
845-1890

(b) Wine ewer
Silver
Hallmarks for London 1848-9, maker's mark of Joseph and
Albert Savory (A.B. Savory and Sons)
Inscribed: 'HARTLEPOOL REGATTA 1848'
H. 30.5cms. W. 15.9cms.
Circ 324-1959

28
Tea and coffee service
Silver, partly gilt and enamelled
Hallmarks for London 1850-51, maker's mark of Joseph
Angell
H. 32.5cm. (of coffee pot)
M.27-c-1883
This service was exhibited in the Great Exhibition of 1851 and
the maker was awarded a Prize Medal by the Jury for
enamelled wares. The two-coloured, translucent enamelling is
a revival of a medieval technique. It was virtually the first
secular example by an English manufacturer, imitating the
work of leading Parisian goldsmiths, which had been greatly
admired and envied in England for the previous decade.

29
Inkstand
Silver
Hallmarks for London 1845-6; maker's mark of Robert
Hennell
L. 21cms. W. 20cms. H. 11cms.
Circ 325-d-1959
The design is based on a mid-18th-century Dutch original.

emphasis on its decorative rather than its formal qualities.

The most prominent firm during this period were the Royal Goldsmiths, Rundell, Bridge and Rundell who dominated the market virtually until the point of their dissolution in 1842, and whose success influenced the direction of the major silversmithing firms until late in the century. Their finances were initially secured by dealing in jewellery from French aristocratic refugees. Both the senior partners, Phillip Rundell and John Bridge, had served their apprenticeship with a jeweller named Rodgers in Bath. Neither had any appreciable experience in a plate manufacturing workshop and the firm first subcontracted their silverwork, and then established two workshops, the first at Lime Kiln Lane, Greenwich, managed by Benjamin Smith and his several associates, and the second in Dean Street, Soho, directed by Paul Storr. Following the practice of Josiah Wedgwood, the potter, the partners employed artists of high repute. The sculptor, William Theed RA, even became a partner in the firm, until his death in 1817. John Flaxman (1755-1826) worked for both Wedgwoods and Rundell's. Others included Thomas Stothard (1755-1834), Edward Hodges Baily (1788-1867) and J B Papworth (1775-1847) who was later, briefly, to become the first Director of the Government Schools of Design.

Rigid control was maintained over the designs which were often executed at one or other of the firm's workshops. But Smith broke with the firm in 1814, after which all manufacturing responsibility passed to Storr. He was made a partner in the Rundell firm in 1811, or earlier, but he in turn severed his connections with Rundell's in 1819 setting up independently. Interestingly the artistic quality of Rundell's output did not noticeably decline.

Rundell's themselves retained control of not only the designs but also possession of the casting moulds. The fashion for cast silver required the production of many intricate moulds which inevitably necessitated substantial capital investment. In order to defray costs the moulds were used a number of times in a variety of different combinations which accounts for similarities between certain pieces produced by the firm.

By the end of the second decade of the century, the range of Rundell's designs had become extraordinarily diverse. Eclecticism, so often associated in the public mind with Victorian work, had its true origin in the Regency. The Antiquarian movement, under which neo-classicism flourished in the early 19th century, had also stimulated the revival of other historical styles. Rundell's appointment as Royal Goldsmiths to George III and his family had given them access to the Royal Collections; their mastery of the rococo style was achieved by studying and extending the service of plate supplied by

Nicholas Sprimont to Frederick, Prince of Wales. Storr, during his association with Rundells, executed designs in the baroque, rococo and neo-classical styles with equal fluency. His set of candlesticks, bearing his mark for 1814 and made for the Duke of Cumberland, bears comparison with the work of Paul de Lamerie (see plate 25). Flaxman, unexpectedly, produced a neo-gothic design for a silver-gilt and jewelled cup supplied by John Bridge to George IV as part of the Grand Service in 1826 (see plate 26).

The success of such bravura pieces by Rundell's had two important effects on 19th-century silversmithing. The increasing uses of naturalistic ornament, derived both from the classical treatment of acanthus leaves and the picturesque use of rococo, floral and plant motifs, encouraged a progressively less stylised form of naturalism which by the 1840s had emerged as its own style in the early Victorian period; in its application to silver, it was used with varying success. The Weymouth Regatta Cup of 1827 by Emes and Barnard has naturalistic ornament deployed on a neo-classical form in a whimsical fashion. Equally incongruous is the ewer made by the London firm of silversmiths, A B Savory and Sons, for the Hartlepool Regatta in 1848, where an embossed maritime scene at the vessel's throat is incorporated unsatisfactorily within an overall rococo treatment (plate 27).

At its fullest development, naturalism dictated the form as well as the decoration of the object, and on a small scale, such as the inkstand by Robert Hennell of London, dated 1845-6, the result could be charming (see plate 29). However, naturalism was also favoured for the grandiose pieces of presentation plate which enjoyed particular favour during the middle of the 19th century, and where the treatment was often exaggerated.

This elaborate sculptural silver popularised by Rundell's, and taken up by their successors, relied on a high degree of figurative realism for its success. These predominantly prestige productions by the major silversmithing firms were regarded with great popular acclaim in the national press, if not always with critical esteem by the cognoscenti. An anonymous writer in the *Journal of Design* for 1850 (Vol. III, p.41) complained that 'all beauty of form ... is lost in the glitter of the metal where burnishing is employed. If ... not burnished, the metal is sacrificed to the art and its value thrown away to no purpose.' Such criticism was not without justification. Not all artists were acquainted with the limitations of silversmithing and their designs did not always translate well in practice.

The Hawkesley Testimonial by Hunt and Roskell, the successors to Paul Storr, is a typical, if late, example (see plate 32). It was presented to Thomas Hawkesley (1807-

30
(a) Three decanter stoppers
Silver
Hallmarks for London 1855-6; maker's mark of Steven Smith
and William Nicholson
Designed by J.C. Horsley ARA (1817-1903) and originally
made by Benjamin Smith Jnr. for Summerley Art Manufactures in 1848
H. 11.4cms. Diam. 4cms.
794-796, 1864

(b) Christening mug
Silver
Hallmarks for London 1865-6; maker's mark for Harry
Emmanuel
Designed by Richard Redgrave RA (1804-88)
Originally made by S.H. & D. Gass for Summerley Art
Manufactures in 1849 and exhibited at the Great Exhibition of
1851
H. 12cms. W. 10cms.
371-1865
Despite Cole's closure of his Summerley venture in 1849, some
designs proved enduringly successful and were subsequently
adopted by other manufacturers.

93) by the directors of the Nottingham Waterworks
Company in 1880 to honour his fifty years of service as
Engineer-in-Chief. Hunt and Roskell were perhaps the
last London manufacturers to produce especially commissioned testimonial plate with any frequency, and this
particular example displays many of the problems inherent in such productions.

The technical execution is faultless but the design
betrays evidence of indecisiveness. Naturalistic ornament adorns an essentially neo-classical framework.
Aquatic botanica abounds amidst mythical and historical
figures, while the salver itself is engraved with six highly
realistic views of Hawkesley's work. But at least in
this instance, the geometric structure dominates. Earlier
testimonials of the 1840s and 1850s were less disciplined.

The painter, Richard Redgrave, was particularly viru-
lent in his condemnation of silver statuary with its obsess-
ive fascination for detail, and his observations reflected
the consensus of opinion within the Society of Arts. This
was an institution, founded in 1754, which sought to
encourage manufacturing and commercial interests in
the Arts. It had, however, become moribund until a
change in its constitution and the appointment of Prince
Albert, the husband of Queen Victoria, as its president in
1843 revived its effectiveness.

The Prince Consort was in few respects like George
IV, but he did have in common an enthusiastic and
enlightened appreciation of the arts. He was concerned,
like many intellectuals of the day, with the declining aesthetic standards in the manufacturing industries. This
had already been the subject of a Parliamentary Select
Committee set up in 1835 and the Prince, in agreement
with their recommendations, sought through the Society
to put them into effect. In this he was very ably assisted by
Henry Cole who was recruited to the Society in 1846.

31

(a) Decanter
Chinese sang-de-boeuf vase, mounted
in silvergilt and decorated with semi-
precious stones, some of them Persian
seals.
No hallmarks c 1870
Designed by William Burges for his
own collection in 1867
Given in memory of Charles and
Lavinia Handley Read by their family
H. 28cm. W. 14cm.
M.22-1972

(b) Drinking cup
Silver, partly gilt, set with semi-
precious stones and enamel
Hallmarks for London 1863-4;
maker's mark of Joseph Hart & Son
Designed by William Burges for
James Nicholson
H. 12.1cm. Diam. 10.8cm.
Circ 858-1956

(c) Soup plate
Silver, with an engraved medallion of
a startled hare
Hallmarks for Birmingham 1867-8;
maker's mark of John Hardman & Co
Designed by William Burges for John
Patrick Crichton Stuart, 3rd

Marquess of Bute
Given by Thomas Lumley
Diam. 27.5cms.
M.59.1981

(d) Decanter
Green glass mounted in silver, partly
gilt, set with amethysts and opals
amongst other semi-precious stones,
and Greek and Roman coins
Hallmarks for London 1865-66;
maker's mark of Richard Green.
Designed by William Burges and
made for James Nicholson
H. 27.9cm. Diam. 17.8cm.
Circ 857-1956

32 (*opposite*)
The Hawkesley Testimonial
Centrepiece, salver and two dessert
stands with engraved glass dishes
Silver, subsequently gilt at the request
of the recipient
Hallmarks for London 1880-81;
maker's mark of John Samuel Hunt
and Robert Roskell, of Hunt and
Roskell
Inscribed with a dedication to
Thomas Hawkesley RCE, FRS, and
the names of the subscribers
H. 73.5 cms. (of centrepeice) Diam.
50.6cms. (of salver)
Given by Mrs T.E. Hawkesley, the
daughter-in-law of Thomas
Hawkesley
M.4-j-1974
This testimonial was presented to
Thomas Hawkesley by his fellow
directors of the Nottingham Waterworks Company: 'In acknowledge-
ment of his eminent services as their
Engineer in Chief from the
commencement of the undertaking
AD 1830 to the dissolution of the
Company AD 1880 (a period of 50
years) and in lasting testimony of their
high personnal regard'.
Hawkesley was the first engineer to
supply continuous running water to
many British cities and towns. His
work on over 150 engineering schemes
in London and other places contributed largely to the eradication of
cholera. His practice was world wide.

33
Jug and two beakers
Silver, partly gilt, decorated with
matting and engraving in the Japanese
taste
Hallmarks for Birmingham 1882-3 (on
all three pieces); maker's mark of
Frederick Elkington; production or
design numbers 15892 on the jug, 11463
on the beakers; the stamp of ELKINGTON
& CO. on all three pieces
The jug inscribed 'PRESENTED TO MISS
KEEN on the occasion of her marriage BY
THE COMBINED STAFF OF THE Patent Nut
and Bolt Compy Limtd WITH THEIR
EARNEST WISHES FOR HER HEALTH AND
HAPPINESS JUNE 26th 1883'
H. 32cms. W. 13cms. (jug)
H. 13cms. W. 7cms. (beakers)
M.45-b-1972
Exhibited in the Victorian and
Edwardian Decorative Art Exhibition

(The Handley Read Collection) at The
Royal Academy, 1972. Catalogue No.
D121-123.
Elkingtons of Birmingham were one of
the first manufacturers to produce
silverware in a Japanoiserie style.
Tiffany's of New York stimulated
Elkingtons and a few other firms by
their experiments with textured silver,
embellished with base metals, which
imitated traditional Japanese metalwork. However the strict British hall-
marking laws prevented the application
of base metals to silver. Some silversmiths circumvented this by submitting
their work for assay before completion
and adding the base metal decoration
later.

34
(a) Egg steamer
Silver with an ebony handle
Hallmarks for Sheffield, 1884-5; maker's mark for
H. Stratford
Design attributed to Dr Christopher Dresser (1834-1904)
H. 20cms. L. 16cms.
M.25-1971

(b) Claret jug
Clear glass with silver mounts
No hallmarks; maker's mark for Hukin and Heath, the
underside of the lid stamped: 'Designed by Dr. C. Dresser'
and with a diamond shaped registration mark indicating that
the design was registered by Hukin and Heath on the 26th
March 1879
H. 24.2cms. W. 16cms.
Circ 186-1966

The Select Committee endeavoured to accommodate the design needs of industry with the view to increasing its economic competitiveness in world markets. Implicit was the assumption that the quality of design was of fundamental importance, and that a certain degree of state intervention was necessary in achieving this. These were radical ideas and did at least make some attempt to come to grips with the problems posed by a rapidly evolving industrial society. One of the most useful mea- sures to arise from such thinking was the legislation enacted in 1842 which ensured legal copyright of manu- facturers' designs, and which therefore encouraged manufacturers to invest in the designs of their products.

However, the Committee generally held the convic- tion that good industrial design could be created out of the craft traditions of the Regency. The silversmithing industry in the 19th century enjoyed an anomalous status, never wholly mechanised or wholly craft except for the specialist end of the market. The Committee's over- whelming nostalgia for the success of Rundell's, and the methods by which this was achieved, prevented them from formulating truly original solutions to the problems of design reform. Most members equated style with surface decoration based on correct archaeological models. The form of the object was given relatively little attention.

This concept of correctness extended to ethical judge- ments being made about the suitability of the styles themselves. Those with strong national and intellectual traditions, such as the Gothic or renaissance, were regarded as pure and hence approved while others, for example the rococo which was considered frivolous and insubstantial, were seen as debased and hence suspect. This association of moral values with aesthetic criteria gave rise to that curious feature of early and mid- Victorian design, 'the battle of the styles'. This spawned much debate of a fiercely partisan nature where the

35
(a) Bowl and cover
Silver and enamel with a stone set finial
Hallmarks for London 1899-1900; maker's mark of
C.R. Ashbee
Given by Miss Mary Adam
Circ 77 and a-1953
Although the bowl bears the mark of Ashbee himself rather
than that of his Guild of Handicraft, he was the designer, not
the executant.

(b) Bowl and cover
Silver and enamel set with a cabochon
Hallmarks for London 1900-01; maker's mark of the Guild of
Handicraft
The bowl embossed with the initials E.F.S.I.
Designed by C.R. Ashbee
H. 10cms. W. 27cms.
M.144 and a-1972
Exhibited 'Victorian and Edwardian Decorative Art (The
Handley Read Collection), Royal Academy 1972. Catalogue
No E66.

J B Papworth, a former associate of Rundell's. They were
intended to educate an artisan class to be fully conversant
with correct historical ornament; but the anticipated
fusion between a fine art education and applied arts
training was compromised by the recalcitrance of the
Royal Academy whose members believed themselves to
have the monopoly on fine arts education, and who
therefore steadfastly refused to co-operate in the new
venture. Consequently, manufacturers failed to have
confidence in the new schools, and by the mid-1840s they
were suffering increasing criticism, not least of all from
Cole and his circle.

Cole was a brilliant administrator with a shrewd and
unrivalled appreciation for the value of good publicity.
He, and his colleagues on the Society of Arts, broadly
accepted the Select Committee's recommendations and
sought to put them into practice. To this end he promoted
a series of trade exhibitions which culminated with the
outstanding success of the Great Exhibition of 1851. The
profits from this in turn led to the establishment of the
South Kensington Museum, the ancestor of the V&A,
and Cole was appointed as its first director. He was also
put in charge of the Schools of Design. His authority was
now supreme and he set about establishing the one and
reforming the other with revolutionary zeal. Cole's success was a result of his passionate belief in the ability of
museums and exhibitions to raise standards of public
taste, and he contributed substantially to establishing

merits of particular styles were passionately advocated to
the detriment of others, and helps explain the rapidly
changing allegiances amongst many intellectuals.

The practical recommendations of the Select Committee led to the establishment of the Government
Schools of Design in 1837, under the initial direction of

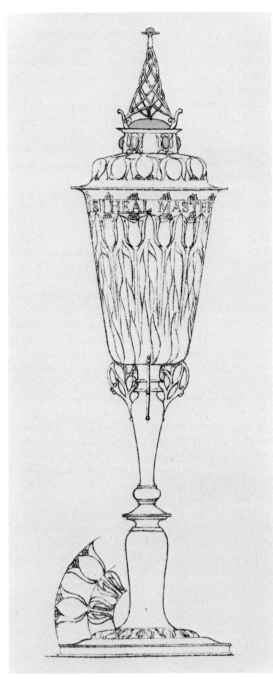

36 (*opposite*)
(a) Cup and cover (The Painter and Stainer's Cup)
Silver set with semi-precious stones and enamelled decoration
Hallmarks for London 1900-01; maker's mark for W. Poyser
Designed by C.R. Ashbee (1863-1942)
H. 44.5cm. W. 12cm.
M.106 and a-1966

Ashbee occasionally went outside the Guild for the execution of his designs and appears to have done so in the case of this cup. Poyser cannot be traced in the Ashbee papers or in the list of Guild workers given in Ashbee's *Craftsmanship in Competitive Industry* 1908.
The cup was commissioned in 1900 by Harris Heal to commemorate his terms of office as Master of the Painters and Stainers Company.

(b) Butter dish
Silver set with a semi-precious stone
Hallmarks for London 1900-01; maker's mark of the Guild of Handicraft Ltd.
Designed by C.R. Ashbee
Given by the Duchess of Leeds
H. 11.2cm. L. 20cm.
Circ 351-1959

(c) Decanter
Green glass with silver mounts, the finial set with a crysoprase
Hallmarks for London 1904-05; maker's mark of the Guild of Handicraft
The glass made by James Powell and Son, Whitefriars, London
H. 22.5cm. W. 16.5cm.
M.121-1966

(d) Design for a cup and cover
C.R. Ashbee: *Modern English Silverwork*, Plate 65, 1909
Lithograph, hand coloured
32 × 23cms.
Library 86 D.D.4

both. His weakness, like his predecessors, lay in his inability to understand satisfactorily what constituted good industrial design.

His 'Felix Summerly' venture (Cole's own pseudonym for his extra-curricular activity) of the late 1840s highlights this. This scheme was intended to show that Cole could effectively translate the recommendations of the Select Committee into practice, while the officially appointed Schools of Design were demonstrating only too clearly their failure to stimulate good design within industry. His formula was simple. He commissioned contemporary artists, some of them already of considerable stature such as Daniel Maclise, Richard Redgrave, J C Horsley and Matthew Digby Wyatt, to produce designs according to criteria laid down by Cole; once vetted by a committee, those approved were subsequently passed to a selected group of manufacturers. The committee's guidelines sought to equate 'the best art with familiar objects in daily use'. Each article was to display 'superior utility' which was not to be sacrificed to ornament. The decoration itself was to exhibit 'appropriate details relating to its use'; a literary rather than visual conception but very characteristic of the time. The examples shown in plate 30 illustrate these principles well enough. The ornament on the christening mug by Richard Redgrave needs no explanation. J C Horsley's set of three decanter stoppers uses vine and grape motifs which was scarcely original since Rundell's had used the same device to decorate decanters in the early years of the century. The use of naturalistic ornament was Cole's gesture towards fashionable taste which he deeply regretted after witnessing the riot of organic naturalism in the 1851 Exhibition.

These designs have charm but are hardly radical. The lack of sufficient experimentation perhaps helped hasten the demise of the Summerly scheme. There were other, more practical, reasons. In order to save his costs, Cole required the manufacturer to take on all the risks of production in addition to paying a royalty for the design on each article produced. This not unnaturally met with stiff protests from even the most enthusiastic supporters, and many manufacturers withdrew complaining that the contractual obligations made the articles prohibitively expensive.

Another of Cole's practices, motivated by economy, was to use the same design for several different media. This only shows how lamentably ignorant he and his associates were of manufacturing processes, and the idiosyncrasies of the materials used. A design which was perfectly satisfactory in silver did not necessarily translate well into ceramic; and moreover several of the designs proposed by Summerly's proved to be hopelessly uneconomic in practice because of the number of dies that would have been required. For these reasons, the Summerly venture declined and by 1849 Cole quietly buried it under the pretext of his preparations for the forthcoming 1851 Exhibition.

Cole did not have a strongly analytical mind and he failed to see the inconsistencies in the Select Committee's policies. He never fully appreciated the dichotomy between craft and industrial manufacture, and that the chosen medium itself imposed design constraints. Later, he did much to popularise the embossed silverwork of Morel Ladeuil and Antoine Vechte in the 1850s and 1860s, (partly to undermine the prevailing taste for testimonials), and in this he was successful. But these elaborately executed pieces, intended primarily for major international exhibitions, bore very little relevance to the output of the firms who commissioned them, and inevitably their production, although exhibiting superb craftsmanship, became repetitive and sterile.

Cole's major mistake however was his failure to appreciate the strength of the medieval movement. He knew and admired A W N Pugin, and secured several examples of his metalwork for the new South Kensington Museum from the Great Exhibition (see front cover). Pugin was a gifted antiquary and a designer of genuine originality. His book, *The True Principles of Pointed Architecture*, published in 1841, was a passionate advocacy of Gothic art, where he sought to analyse its qualities according to fundamental principles of architectural and ornamental design. Pugin's concepts of ornamental propriety and harmonious proportions struck a responsive chord in Cole, but he failed to recognise that Pugin not only advocated a revival of medieval design, but a return to medieval craftsmanship which ran directly counter to the Industrial Revolution. This was further elaborated by the critic John Ruskin whose writings inspired William Morris, in the 1860s, to abandon his architectural studies for the practice of the crafts. Many who were to develop into leading designers of the late 19th century associated themselves with Morris rather than Cole and ultimately established the Arts and Crafts movement.

Pugin's knowledge of Gothic architecture and ornament was principally derived from late-14th and 15th-century English medieval art. William Burges, perhaps the most antiquarian of the High Victorian Gothicists, developed an increasing preference for earlier, Continental, precedents. The son of an engineer, Burges trained as an architect in the offices of Edward Blore and Matthew Digby Wyatt. By the 1860s he had acquired an international reputation as a medieval archaeologist. His principal interest was in French Gothic art of the 13th century, but he also drew inspiration from Italian, Arabic, Japanese, Pompeian and Assyrian sources. He was fascinated in particular by the Islamic permeation of Gothic medieval art. Nowhere is this better exemplified than in his designs for metalwork (see plate 31) where the green glass decanter in particular incorporates precious and exotic fragments such as Greek coins, Chinese jade and Persian seals. Towards the end of his brief career (he died in 1881 at the age of 53) Burges became increasingly convinced that the future and salvation of architecture depended on a renaissance of the decorative arts, and for this reason he is often regarded as an important forerunner of the Arts and Crafts movement itself.

The 1860s saw the climax of the Gothic revival but also the seeds of revolt. A new generation began to emerge who started to question the necessity for a moral imperative in the choice of styles. By the 1870s aestheticism, or 'art for art's sake', often associated with Oscar Wilde and his circle, was becoming increasingly attractive to a young middle class public. Nationalistic attitudes in the use of ornament fell out of favour. Exotic cultures and, in particular, the arts of Japan, increasingly dominated the public imagination. This had its own measure of frivolity as can be seen by commercial attempts to capitalise on the fashion (see plate 33) but it had serious aspects too. One of the most gifted designers of the latter part of the 19th century, Christopher Dresser, executed his most enterprising designs in metalwork after his return from an extended visit to Japan in 1876.

Dresser was a student at the Government Schools of Design during the late 1840s and early 1850s and was strongly influenced by the teaching of Richard Redgrave and Owen Jones. Their vigorous emphasis on the need to conventionalise motifs, and their insistence that the designers' task was to regard the utilitarian qualities of the object as of overriding importance, were to dominate Dresser's attitude to design for the rest of his life. Redgrave taught him botanical drawing and such was Dresser's enthusiasm for the subject that in 1860 he was awarded an honorary doctorate from the University of Jena for his botanical research. He published a series of articles in the *Art Journal* which discussed plant structure and its relation to design. Dresser was later to argue that his metalwork designs evolved according to 'natural laws'. A more obvious influence was the restrained simplicity of Japanese metalwork but it would be unwise to attribute his designs at any stage entirely to his liking for Japanese objects. Many of his highly original shapes arose out of a dual concern with the techniques of mass production and with the function of the articles he designed (plate 34).

In contrast to Dresser's commitment to mass production the Arts and Crafts movement, under the guidance of William Morris, pursued the virtues of craft handwork. The crafts, which had been neglected for half a century, suddenly, under Morris's influence, became a respectable pursuit. This movement, inspired by the doctrines of Ruskin, was imbued with the romantic conception of medieval craftsmanship as a golden age existing in the days of pre-industrial production.

One of the most energetic and idealistic men to be attracted to this idea was Charles Robert Ashbee who established the Guild of Handicraft in 1888. It was intended as a co-operative venture, designed to encourage the full creative potential of the craftsman as well as to be an experiment in social democracy. Ashbee emphasised the need for a fully integrated approach. The designer should be knowledgeable of the craftsman's skills and work alongside him; the craftsman himself should be fully conversant with all aspects of his trade. The products of the metalwork workshops in the Guild's early days show a distinctly amateurish quality. Ashbee himself, trained as an architect, had no metalwork experience and he was reluctant to recruit members of the trade in case they corrupted the others by their ex-

perience. After some initial fumbling, the Guild, by the late 1890s, had evolved a mature and distinctive style. Its distinguishing characteristics were holloware with softly planished surfaces, decorated with chasing, embossing and flat areas of enamel and set with semi-precious stones. Handles, feet and finials, instead of being cast as with earlier examples, were now formed of elegant wirework. There is evidence at times of historical precedent. Ashbee regarded the study of 17th-century English and Continental goldsmiths' work in particular as an essential part of the Guild's programme of self-education, but even in the most obvious examples where an historical prototype has been adapted, such as the Painter and Stainers cup (see plate 36), the result is a very contemporary and subtle restatement of the original design.

In the early years of this century, the Guild enjoyed a moderate prosperity but it was short lived, undermined by Ashbee's perfectionism and the plagiarism of his designs by more commercially minded firms such as Liberty's. When the lease expired on the Guild's London premises in 1908, he moved it to Chipping Camden in the Cotswolds, but the removal of the Guild from the proximity to its main market proved financially disastrous and in 1907 Ashbee was reluctantly forced to begin winding up its affairs.

The firm of Liberty and Company of Regent Street represented the most successful exploitation of the Arts and Crafts movement. They initiated their 'Cymric' range of silverware in 1899, which was principally manufactured by W H Hasler and Company of Birmingham. The most distinctive style claimed Celtic inspiration but it also owed much to the experiments of Ashbee and, to a lesser extent, the influence of Continental Art Nouveau. They employed some very able designers. These included Archibald Knox, a Manxman introduced to the firm by Christopher Dresser, Bernard Cuzner and Rex Silver (see plate 37). Other members of the movement who deserve a mention include Alexander Fisher, an enamellist who seems to have taught most of his distinguished contemporaries, his pupil Nelson Dawson, founder and associate of the Artificers Guild, and Henry Wilson who produced comparatively few but some of the most imaginative pieces of domestic plate of the Edwardian era.

The influence of the Arts and Crafts movement dwindled on into the inter-war years. Liberty's only wound up their production of the Cymric range of silverware in 1927, by which time it was well and truly out of fashion. Some designers, although educated in the Arts and Crafts tradition, were able to adapt their work to changing tastes. Amongst the most successful at doing so were H G Murphy and Harold Stabler. Murphy, who before the

37
(a) Candlestick
Silver
Hallmarks for Birmingham 1906-07;
maker's mark of Liberty and Company
(Cymric) Ltd.
Designed by Rex Silver (1879-1965)
H. 24.5cm. Diam. 14.5cm.
Circ 165-1969
Illustrated in the *The Studio*, Vol XIX,
1900.

(b) Biscuit box
Silver, decorated with enamel and
mother of pearl
Hallmarks for Birmingham 1901-02;
maker's mark of Liberty and Co
(Cymric) Ltd.
Design attributed to Archibald Knox
(1864-1933)
H. 19cms. W. 9cms. L. 13cms.
M.25-1972
Exhibited 'Victorian and Edwardian
Decorative Art' (The Handley Read
Collection), Royal Academy 1972.
Catalogue No E96

(c) Cup and cover
Silver, set with enamels and opals, gilt
interior
Hallmarks for Birmingham 1901-02;
maker's mark of Liberty and Co
(Cymric) Ltd.
Designed by Archibald Knox
H. 23cm. Diam. 13cm.
M.304 and a-1975

38 (*opposite*)
(a) Loving cup and cover
Silver, decorated with painted enamel and moonstones, the
stem of ivory
No hallmarks, c 1905-1909
Designed and made by Harold Stabler (1872-1945)
Inscribed: 'DRINK AND FEAR NOT YOUR MAN'
H. 26.5cms. W. 12cms.
Given by Miss M. McLeish
Circ 501-1956

(b) Cup and Cover
Silver, the cover decorated with enamel representing
nasturtiums and a stone set finial
Hallmarks for London 1903-04; maker's mark and the enamel
signed by Nelson Dawson
H. 23.5cms. W. 14cms.
M.30 and a-1968

First World War had produced richly embellished plate to Henry Wilson's designs, in the 1920s produced silverware of classical simplicity, often decorated with highly competently executed engraving which had not been a technique favoured by the Arts and Crafts metalworkers.

Stabler first gained his metalworking experience at the Keswick School of Industrial Art and before the War produced such pieces as the cup illustrated in plate 38, embellished in the standard Arts and Crafts manner using mounted stones and painted enamels. He was a founder member of the Design and Industries Association which was established in 1915 as an action group intended to promote modern design. At first dominated by members of the Arts and Crafts movement, it had by the 1930s become intimately involved with the promotion of the Modern Movement. Stabler's sensitivity to modern trends is reflected in his design of a tea set for Adie Brothers of Birmingham in the mid 1930s (see plate 39) which is entirely geometric in character and typical of the 'Art Deco' style, fashionable at the time. Stabler proved to be

39
Tea service
Silver, the handles and knops of wood and ivory
Birmingham hallmarks for 1935-6; maker's mark of Adie Brothers Ltd. The underside stamped 'Stabler' in script and 'REG. APPLIED FOR'
Designed by Harold Stabler
L.(overall) 19.8cms. W. 7.6cms. H. 8.3cms. (of teapot)
M.291-c-1976
Illustrated in the *Studio Year Book of Decorative Arts*, 1938 p.118.
A version of this design was also produced by the same company in electroplate.

39

40
(a) Tea service
Silver, partly gilt
Hallmarks for London 1950-51; special mark of the Festival of
Britain, maker's mark Leslie Durbin. (The tongs, 1982, recast
from the original moulds by Leslie Durbin)
Designed by Robert Goodden, CBE, RDI (b.1909), for the
Royal Pavilion at the Festival of Britain. Inscribed
with couplets composed by R. Gooden
Made by Leslie Durbin, MVO, LL D (b.1913)
The sugar tongs donated by Leslie Durbin
H. 25.7cms. (hot water jug)
M.176-c-1976; M.80-1982
This service was used by King George VI and Queen
Elizabeth at the opening of the Festival in May 1951.
Robert Goodden, the nephew of the silversmith R.M.Y.
Gleadowe, was initially trained as an architect at the Architec-
tural Association, but began to design silverware while still a
student. He took a prominent part in the preparations for the
Festival of Britain on the South Bank, where he designed the
Lion and Unicorn Pavilion. He was Professor of Silver-
smithing at the Royal College of Art from 1948 to 1974.

Leslie Durbin who was trained at the Central School, was a
distinguished silversmith who undertook many commissions
for corporation plate.

(b) Design for the handle of a cream jug from the tea service
made for the Royal Pavilion at the Festival of Britain, 1951
Pencil
20 × 7cms.
E149-1977

(a) 'Saddleback' teapot
Silver – no hallmarks
Designed by Gerald Benney and made in his London
workshop
H. 14cms. Max. L. 17.6cm.
M.85-1979
This teapot was made for a limited competition in 1961,
sponsored by the Ministry of Public Buildings and Works for
a silver service to be made for the use of British Embassies
abroad. The competition was limited to two; the other
candidate being David Mellor. Both of them worked up
designs but Mellor's proposals were preferred by the selection
committee and after the prototype stage, Benney's designs
were dropped.

(b) Jug
Silver, the inside gilt, the exterior of the body decorated with
black enamel, the handle carved ivory
Hallmarks for London 1978, sponsors mark of Gerald Benney,
craftman's work of Alan Evans
Designed by Gerald Benney and made in his workshop at
Beenham House near Reading, Berkshire
H. 17.8cms. W. 23cms.
M.166-1978
This is the first piece of silver to be commissioned by the
V&A.
The body of the jug represented the largest area enamelled in
Benney's workshop.

an able designer in other media. He designed cermics for
the Poole pottery, which included tiles for the London
Underground, and he designed a series of prototypes for
Firth Vickers, the Sheffield stainless steel manufacturers.
J.J. Wiggan of Walsall was one of the very few English
companies to respond to his initiative, and put into production Stabler's Cumberland tea set in 1938 and continued its manufacture until the early 1960s.

The role of the silversmith as an industrial designer
was to prove increasingly important in the 1950s. Three
major silversmiths who began their careers after the
Second World War spent some of the early years of their
working lives as consultant designers to major Sheffield
firms. Gerald Benney designed a martini pitcher and
accompanying tankards for Viners; Robert Welch the
Campden range for J J Wiggins and David Mellor the
Pride teaset and range of cutlery for Walker and Hall. All
these products won Design Awards from the Council of
Industrial Design which had been established in 1944 by
the wartime government under the chairmanship of
Gordon Russell, in order to stimulate the expected post-
war industrial recovery. This activity represented the
apotheosis of Cole's ambitions of the previous century,
trained craftsmen working for industry, and to some
extent the credit for this is due to Cole's initial achievements. But it is also a reflection of the crude economic

41

42
Pair of candelabra
Silver
Hallmarks for London 1980; maker's mark of Robert Welch
Inscribed: 'TENEBRAS FUGO:OCULOS LAETOR:NOCTEM CORONANS
R.S. ME FIERI FECIT: V&A 1980' (I put darkness to flight, rejoice
the eyes, crowning the night. R(oy) S(trong) had me made:
V&A 1980)
H. 38cms. W. 31.5cms.
M.61&a-1980

Commissioned by the Museum for its permanent collections.
Robert Welch was born in 1929 and trained at the Birmingham
School of Art under Ralph Baxendale and Cyril Shiner. From
1952 to 1955 he was at the Royal College of Art, after which he
was appointed, as design consultant, to J.J. Wiggin of
Sheffield. Throughout his career he has undertaken many
industrial design commissions (he designed the stainless steel
tableware for the Orient liner, 'Oriana') while continuing to
practise as a silversmith. He has undertaken several prestige
commissions for Goldsmiths' Hall

reality facing silversmiths today. The ravages of two major world wars this century has eroded much of the traditional support for the silversmithing trade. Even the most accomplished and senior members of the craft nowadays find it difficult to survive without diversifying their activities.

43
Bowl
Silver with gold details
Designed and made by Rod Kelly
Hallmarked 1984
Donated by Dairy Crest Industrial Products, a division of the Milk Marketing Board.
H. 7.5cms. Diam. 19cms.
M.74-1984
Rod Kelly did his initial training at Birmingham Polytechnic where he gained a degree in Three Dimensional Design. He continued his education with post graduate work in the School of Silversmithing and Jewellery at the Royal College of Art, graduating in 1983.

The Goldsmith's Company deserves particular mention in its continuing efforts to counteract these influences. In 1925 it began its own collection of contemporary silversmiths' work and through a vigorous programme of exhibitions, involvement in trade fairs and awarding of scholarships has emerged as one of the leading patrons of their craft. The help it has given to contemporary silversmiths has been invaluable. For example it was G R Hughes, the Clerk of the Company, who introduced Harold Stabler to Firth Vickers and more recently the Company supervised many of the commissions for insignia required by the new universities set up in the 1960s. Their enlighted example has actively encouraged others to follow. Recently the V&A has started commissioning pieces for its own collection of Museum plate.

This survey ends with an illustration of the most recently acquired piece of modern plate by the Museum at the time of writing (see plate 43). It was commissioned by the Milk Marketing Board from Rod Kelly, a graduate from the Royal College of Art in 1983, with the intention that it would ultimately form part of a public collection. The sophisticated design and technical execution give every encouragement to a general conviction that the new generation of silversmiths have all the necessary ideas and talent to continue the rich traditions of their forebears.

43

Further Reading

The bibliography of English silver is extensive and the titles suggested below have been selected for their particular relevance to the period covered by this book. Many of them have useful bibliographies themselves.

The following general histories provide a broad coverage of the subject and can be recommended:

C J Jackson *An Illustrated History of English Plate Ecclesiastical and Secular,* illustrated, 2 vols, London, 1911. This has been reprinted in facsimile by Dover Publications, New York, 1969.

Charles Oman, *English Domestic Silver,* illustrated 5th edition, London, 1962.

Charles Oman, *English Silversmiths' Work, Civil and Domestic,* London (HMSO) 1965. This has over 200 black and white illustrations of silver in the collections of the V&A.

Gerald Taylor, *Silver,* illustrated, London, 1956.

Michael Clayton, *The Collector's Dictionary of Gold and Silver,* illustrated, London, 1971. This, as the title itself suggests, is presented as a dictionary rather than in narrative form and is an invaluable reference book for the reader who requires amplification on specific points.

For particular periods, the following series of Faber monographs provide excellent introductions:

Charles Oman, *Caroline Silver,* illustrated, London, 1970.

John Hayward, *Huguenot Silver in England 1688-1727,* illustrated, London, 1959.

Arthur Grimwade, *Rococo Silver,* illustrated, London, 1974.

Robert Rowe, *Adam Silver 1765-1795,* illustrated, London, 1965.

Until relatively recently, Victorian and Modern silver was largely ignored by writers and the general histories mentioned above, with the exception of Clayton, treat these subjects very sketchily if at all. For the reader who is particularly interested in 19th and 20th-century silver, the next three titles provide a very useful background:

Patricia Wardle, *Victorian Silver and Silver-Plate,* illustrated, London, 1963.

John Culme, *Nineteenth Century Silver,* illustrated, London, 1977.

Graham Hughes, *Modern Silver throughout the World 1880-1967,* illustrated, London, 1967.

For more detailed information, the following articles are very highly recommended:

John Hayward, 'Aurifices Regis' (Rundell Bridge and Rundell) *Antiques,* June, 1971 (Part I), July 1971 (Part II)

Shirley Bury, 'The Lengthening Shadow of Rundell's', Part I Rundell's and their Silversmiths, Part II The substance and growth of the Flaxman tradition, Part III The Rundell influence on the Victorian trade *Connoisseur* February, March, April, 1966.

Charles Oman, 'A Problem of Artistic Repsonsibility: The Firm of Rundell Bridge and Rundell', *Apollo,* February 1966.

Shirley Bury 'The Silver Designs of Dr. Christopher Dresser', *Apollo,* December 1962.

Shirley Bury, 'An Arts and Crafts Experiment: The Silverwork of C.R. Ashbee', *Victoria and Albert Museum Bulletin* January 1967.

Shirley Bury, 'The Liberty Metalwork Venture', *The Architectural Review,* February 1963.

Exhibition catalogues provide a definitive coverage of a specific period or, are useful for placing the individual within a broader context. The following are recommended:

Rococo, Art and Design in Hogarth's England, London, V&A, 1984

The Age of Neoclassicism, London Arts Council, 1971.

Victorian and Edwardian Decorative Art, London, Royal Academy, 1952.

Victorian and Edwardian Decorative Art — The Handley-Read Collection, London, Royal Academy, 1972.

C.R. *Ashbee and the Guild of Handicraft*, Cheltenham Art Gallery, 1981.

Liberty's, London, V&A, 1975.

The Worshipful Company of Goldsmiths as Patrons of their Craft 1919-53, London, Goldsmiths' Hall, 1965.

Thirties, London, Arts Council 1979.

The next three titles are definitive monographs on individual makers and are models of their kind:

P A S Phillips, *Paul de Lamerie*, London, 1935

Elaine Barr, *George Wickes*, London, 1980

N M Penzer, *Paul Storr*, London, 1954 (reprinted by Hamlyn's, London 1971).

For information on hallmarks and makers' marks, the following titles are amongst the most informative:

Frederick Bradbury, *Guide to Marks of Origin on British and Irish Silver Plate*, Sheffield (Revised edition published annually).

C.J. Jackson, *English Goldsmiths and their Marks*, 2nd edition, London 1921 (Reprinted most recently by Dover Publications, New York 1964).

Arthur Grimwade, *English Goldsmiths 1697-1837, Their Marks and Lives*, London 1976, revised 1982. This is the most useful reference for identifying makers' marks within the period specified by the title.

Susan Hare, *Touching Gold and Silver; 500 Years of Hallmarks*, illustrated, London 1978. A catalogue of the exhibition held at Goldsmiths' Hall and an excellent introduction to the subject.

Finally, for detailed coverage of silversmithing techniques, the following two titles are recommended:

Henry Wilson, *Silverwork and Jewellery*, London, 1902. (reprinted in paperback by Pitman 1978).

Robert Goodden and Phillip Popham, *Silversmithing*, London 1971.

John Flude

PAWNBROKER and **SILVERSMITH**

No 3 Grace Church Street

London

Lends Money on Plate, Watches, Jewells, Wearing Apparel,
Household Goods, & Stock in Trade.

NB

Goods Sent from any Part of y Country directed as above,
shall be duly attended too & the Utmost Value lent thereon.